Troika IV

ThornTree Press
547 Hawthorn Lane
Winnetka, Illinois, 60093

Printed in the United States of America
First Edition
First Printing

FUNNY HOW YOU REMEMBER THINGS
by Judy Brinkworth

PULLING UP THE DAWN
by Helen Reed

HIDDEN SEED
by Laurel Mills

Cover Art: P. Buckley Moss, **"Horses Three,"** *permission given by the artist*
Typography: Elizabeth Grudzien

A grant from the **Illinois Arts Council** has contributed to this project. *Thorntree Press*, a not-for-profit publisher, acknowledges contributions from friends whose tax-deductible gifts have made this book possible.

ISBN: (Paperback) 0-939395-18-5
Library of Congress Catalog Number: 90-71311

Published in 1992
Thorntree Press
547 Hawthorn Lane
Winnetka, IL 60093

FUNNY HOW YOU REMEMBER THINGS

by

JUDY WREN BRINKWORTH

for my father and mother,
Thomas and Esther Auguste Emilie Stroh Wren

Judy Brinkworth's poetry has been syndicated by the *Chicago Tribune.*

She writes poems that are strong, but tender, evocative yet precise, poems that are just plain lovely. I'm jealous.

– Judy Markey

CONTENTS

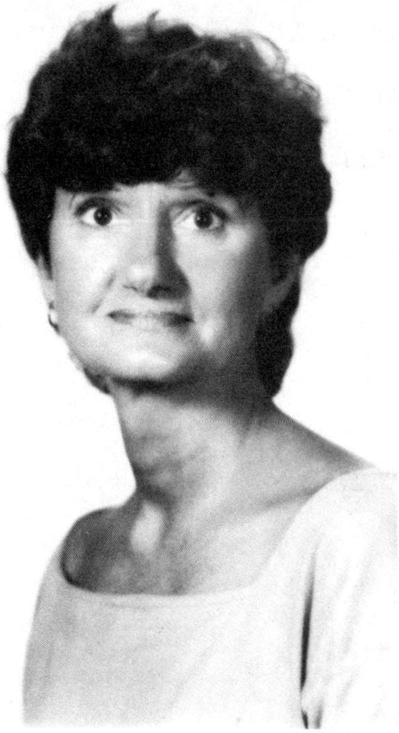

Photo credit: John Howell

Judy Wren Brinkworth lives in Wilmette with her husband and two children. Once upon a time, she was an airline stewardess with TWA. She has a background in public relations.

WHEN SHE WAS 12 AND 7/8, AND I HAD JUST TURNED 10.

Before that pokey summer dawdled down
to crayon buying, the yearly combat
over new school shoes,

> "Mama, when I grow up, all my shoes
> will be red. And flimsy."

What happened was,
my sister Kathy abandoned me.

It was the year of the fans.
Preceded by the year of the potholders,
which followed the year of the
Kleenex carnations. With lipstick edges.
But this was the year we made fans.

Front porch evenings, we'd assemble
our supplies: paper, paint, glitter, glue,
faded-lady Southern drawls.
Kathy chose our names.
"Ruby Faye." "Cordelia Rose."
Fold and pleat, fold and pleat.
Kathy, to the Chicago August night,

> "Just smell that sweet ole' honeysuckle,
> sister dear."
>
> "That's just the macaroni and cheese from dinner."
>
> "Ah said, cain't you just SMELL that sweet ole'
> HONEYSUCKLE, RUBY FAYE!"

Oh. Right.

> "Ah do, ah do, Cordelia Rose. Toooo deevine."

And the damp taffeta air would percolate
with the dainty swish of fans,
used later,
when chiffon breezes slithered through porch railings,
to whack lightning bugs.

"Why, Ruby Faye, looky here who's comin'.
Ah do believe it's Johnny Martin and his sweetheart.
Appears she's had one slice too many of pecan pie.
Not to mention shortnin' bread."

Behind the fans, our whispers picked apart
all the neighbors who meandered by.
Especially older girls.
Especially older girls with boyfriends.
We sat, politely, 'til they passed,
then rolled our eyes, held our throats,
made gagging noises, and fell over in disgust.

One night, one like all the rest, I thought,
we printed "DAMN" on pink construction paper,
creased it for a fan,
and called my father out,
exploding into giggles as Kathy fluttered
the Forbidden, Hidden Word.

"So? So?"

He shook his head and went inside.

"Marge, when, oh when, does school start?"

Suddenly, I spied a potential victim.

"Hey, here comes Johnny Martin. Alone."

Grabbing a fan, I scrunched down on the step,
waiting for Kathy's jokes to begin.
But Johnny Martin stopped.
He looked at us. He looked at Kathy.
He sauntered over to our porch, said,

"Hi, Blue Eyes,"

to my sister, then slouched on down the block,
whistling.
And I waited for Kathy's jokes to begin.

And I waited for Kathy's jokes to begin.

And something seemed all of a sudden
different. But what?

Kathy got up. Slowly.

"You finish the silly fans, if you want.
I think I'll go in and read for a while."

Read? Kathy? On a summer night?

"Cordelia Rose, don't you dare leave your
sister dear alone here on the verandah!"

I guess I sounded desperate.
She turned, with a smile I hadn't seen before.

"Oh, Ruby Faye, don't get in a tizzy.
Ah'm just goin' upstairs.
Ah'm not a-ban-don-in' you."

But, of course, she was.

SAFETY IN NUMBERS

There she would stand, Miss Foster would,
older than God, but with greater authority,
since God had a habit of not showing up much,
while Miss Foster was there, every Monday through Frid-
ay,
9 to 9:45 a.m. Algebra I.

Had she ever been less than ancient? No.
She probably came with the building, I guessed.
The last brick in place: Miss Foster appeared.
Her Woolworth's Invisible Hairnet intact,
it hovered above her aquarium eyes,
watery blue in steel-rimmed glasses,
they impaled her classes impartially.

She hated us all.

She always had. She did now. She always would.
Miss Foster's loathing was absolute.

It's why I liked being in her room.

I mean, you could count on Miss Foster.
She would always despise you.
Whereas, life in the halls was so chancy.
Popularity? Pimples? Which was yours for the day?
Oh, better the shelter of Miss Foster's wrath.

She Reigned Supreme.

And for forty-five blessed minutes each morning,
I could relax.
"You're all dumb," she yelled, "not just dumb,
DENSE!" My muscles untensed.
Maybe it won't be so bad. High school.
Maybe I'll really fit in, I hoped.
For just like the rest, I was detested!

The thought cheered me up.
So there she would stand, Miss Foster would,
preaching her passion for x's and y's,
using a pointer like a pool shark's cue,
tapping the board, aiming equations
at the empty side pockets of our unworthy minds.

While scrunched in our seats,
and secure in Miss Foster's complete lack of faith in us,
we learned we could face the day.

PROFESSIONAL HELP

The man who replaced the shower door
in the old house we bought after Sarah was born
arrived on time.
Stunned from punctuality,
(a repairman who knew time mattered!)
I rushed him up the stairs, furtively
hurtling toys from his path,
babbling about
our bathroom's inadequacies.

The shower door. A mildewed dilemma
of fractured glass and rusted metal
bolted to an ancient tub.
Our rotting portal. Perpetually off its track
and on my nerves.

"It was like this when we moved in."

But the shower door man ignored my
explanation of this bequest of filth
and surveyed, with narrowed eyes, this...
this offense to his profession.
I held my breath.

"It will take one hour to do. Exactly."

Then, as if stating some eternal truth,

"You shouldn't have to live with this."

I slumped, lightheaded, back
against the sink.
No, I shouldn't.
I definitely should not.
Have to live with this.
Or the awful fulling plaster.

Or the baby's year-long colic.
Or my husband's

> "Just a few suggestions so you can get
> better organized, for God's sake,"

tirade of tips, delivered
every night.

I ran downstairs and raced back up
with a glass (not a jelly jar!)
of 7-UP (with ice), and two
Pepperidge Farm cookies.
On a plate.
I resisted a doily.

While the shower door was worked on,
I folded laundry in a nearby room.
At last, Something Was Being Done Right.
I started humming.
Hadn't done that in months.
Most days I simply listened
to the house decay.

Now I talked. And talked. And,

> "Hey, 'shower door' reminds me of 'cellar door'.
> I saw a woman named 'Cellar Door' once.
> On a re-run of Groucho Marx' old show.
> Prettiest words in the English language.
> That's what her father thought.
> So that's what he named her.
> 'Cellar Door!' Can you imagine?"

Bless his heart, all he replied was,

> "Do tell."

> It was a lovely hour.

And what a door!

"It will never break or go off the track.
Watch."

He shoved it to the other side. It bounced,
with a reverberating hum.

"Much easier to clean, too."

And we smiled at each other,
and then he left.

I went back upstairs and looked at the door,
then slammed it six or seven times
before I woke the baby.

Since then? Well, the plumbing went,
the tile, the marriage too,
which is not surprising, considering
the condition they were in.
The door, however, has endured.

And sometimes,
when I take a shower late at night and,
you know, semi-wonder if I might get
murdered Psycho-like, I console myself
that at least, it won't be messy.

"She bled totally within the tub,
behind the pebbled shower door,
that did not break or leave its track!"

Right there in the Enquirer.

Unless, by chance, the clever fiend
would take the time
and have the talent
to dismantle
the entire door. Oh, blood would flow
most everywhere.

I doubt that this would happen though.

For seldom do you meet a man
who takes such pride
in a job well done.

I met one only once.

COMEUPPANCE

I narrowed in for the kill.

"Well, one thing's for sure,
we won't end up like Irene.
There, I got it!"

An infinitesimal hair quivered
in the silvered grip
of my eyebrow tweezers.

The Saturday morning ritual.
Pondering our prospects and our pores.

"What? No family, no friends,
and an enchanting career at the
checkout counter isn't for you?
Picky, picky," Nancy muttered
through a hole in her oatmeal mask.

And we laughed,

"Oh, God, my entire face just cracked!"

with the smugness and sly contempt
so endearing in 16 year olds.

Irene.
Presiding over the supermarket like
John Wayne in a rowdy barroom,

"She's the fastest checker in the West,
by crackee." (Nancy, doing Gabby Hayes.)

Lowly part-timers, we sulkily watched her
sashay the shoppers through her line.

"Could you check how much that cereal costs?"

Showdown. New customer, poor sap.
Quiet, quiet. All eyes on Irene.

"Certainly, sir," she hisses. "Price check
on 5, Cheerios, small," blares the microphone.

Quiet, quiet. She taps her foot,
studies her fingernails.

"79¢," yells the manager,

"PRECISELY!" yells Irene at the twerp.

He slinks out the door.
She's Numero Uno!
I think I hear someone applaud.

But it was all she had.
She lived alone in a furnished room.
We knew she was old, (at least 35).
No one knew anything else for sure,
except Nancy and I, who loved to imagine
an abysmally dismal existence,
just for Irene.

"There she sits, scrunched in shabby
chenille, guzzling V-8 Juice,
(on Special, 'til Thursday),
quietly sobbing through all night re-runs,
Deteriorating into Eternity."

I bowed my head for effect.

Well, of course, we pitied her!
Nobody to care for, all by herself.
She did one thing well, that's all.

But that was Irene and this was us,
and all that mattered was moving on,
and college and marriage and who knows what,
and anyway, we got fired.

Yet, while it has all been coming true,
I've sometimes thought of Irene.
When computer scanning of groceries came in,
did she retire? Was her register bronzed?
Nancy and I would laugh and remember,
with the smugness and sly contempt
so endearing in 40 year olds.

Until today.
Today in our annual telephone chat,
Nancy seems tired. I sounded harassed.

Her oldest daughter has moved back home.
My son refuses to leave.
Her elderly uncle broke his hip.
My brother's out of a job.
Her mother's health is rapidly failing.
I'm falling behind at work.
Her son's a muddle of teen-age trouble.
My husband's got middle-age angst.

And they all depend on us.

Yes, our lives are full.
In fact, overflowing....

> "Hey, remember Irene? How she lived alone?
> No one to care for, by herself.
> She did one thing well, that's all."

And the words hang between us,
after all these years, not spoken with
smugness, or pity, or contempt,
but with something that's close to,
not too far removed from,
that almost resembles,
envy.

ANDY'S CANDIES

On Winnemac, across from Reverend Axelson's,
stuffed between the fire station and
Bergen's Shoe Repair ("Heels While U Wait"),
if Mr. Bergen feels okay, if he isn't made at life again,
or you, or your Sunday Mary Janes,
that will wait, patiently, toes pointed in,
while he goes off again,
someplace, to be soothed.

But he ignores us now, as we trample into Andy's,
clutching begged nickels, baby-sitting dimes,
squeezing into every inch of store
not tattooed with loot.
What a place!
A tiny cave, barnacled in comic books
and clutter, surrounding Mrs. Reiner
(no "Andy" here, only Mrs. Reiner, always and forever),
who twitters like a soft, grey bird
guarding over her nest:

"Now you kids, stop snapping the gumball machine knob
and, you there, leave those lollipops alone
and decide, for heaven's sake, what you really want,
and, oh, DON'T LEAN ON THE GLASS!"

Standing in the back, waiting for an ice cream cone,
I scrunch my eyes, and the walls
percolate with color,
like in some blurry baby dream, then
underneath the blackboard screech of voices
I hear the fire siren start next door,
and Mr. Bergen yelling at the shoes again,
and it's so hot, and
what if that vaguely stale smell
is not old ice cream but old

Andy, chopped to fool the cops,
frozen long ago...

"Lemme out," I yell,

throwing money down and
myself out through the door,
to gulp the wonderful Winnemac air,
to cross by Reverend Axelson's,
to lurch home, drunk
on Jujubees.

THE BLESSING

I was twelve the week my mother
painted our apartment blue.
I came home to stacks of cans,
tin totem poles,
sitting in our kitchen.
Each shiny column had the same
mysterious inscription
repeated over and over
like some tribal chant:

#31 Lapis Lazuli Latex Flat
#31 Lapis Lazuli Latex Flat
#31 Lapis Lazuli La...

"You're here, hon! Now we can start."

My mother's energy tornadoed through
the room colliding with my sigh
of resignation. What now?
What project, what idea, what
dumb dream had she come up with?
That was supposed to change our lives
forever. That never worked.
I looked over at my father.
Three weeks sober, without a job
or the courage to meet our eyes,
he shrugged, "You know your mom."

Boy, did I.
Alice Amelia Evelyn Dougherty.
Ninety six pounds of pep.
Inhabiting her days like an actress
used to better roles,
she wished away worries,
entered contests, answered want-ads
("Make a Fortune Stuffing Envelopes

at Home!") as if she expected life
to notice all her efforts and give
exact change.

"You'll see, someday our ship will come in."

I saw we were drowning,
with little hope of rescue.

But now, I watched the latest drama
begin. With Michelangelo-majesty,
she christened the kitchen wall
with a Lapis Lazuli swipe.

Navy blue.
Catholic-school-uniform navy blue.
A compulsory color,
not one you'd choose to be around.

"Kind of dark, isn't it?" I asked.
I mean, no one else on the block
has walls that color."

"Since when do we care what anybody else has.
Besides, it's what anybody who's anybody
has this year."

Making perfect sense to herself,
she nodded towards a magazine
lying open on the sink.

An English castle on display.
Echo-chamber rooms.
Here a tapestry, there a treasure.
"Redefining space through an indigo wash,"
the caption read, "the estate's interiors
now glow with an intimate charm."

I looked around our tiny, clutter-crammed
apartment. Any more intimate and
we'd suffocate.
In a blue cocoon.

But I didn't say it.
Or point out the money spent on paint
could have gone for next month's rent.
She said,

"It'll hide the dirt, and
I got it on sale, and
I just know it'll look terrific,"

but all I heard was that same desperate
telephone voice used to convince
the grocer, the electric company, the landlord
that, yes, of course, the check would be
in the mail today, thanks so much for calling.

I grabbed the brush and splattered
a giant exclamation point on the wall.

"Hey, Mom. It'll be great. Let's get started."

We finished the kitchen that night.

II.

When did I begin to think of my parents
as children.

Hansel and Gretal - lost in the woods.

Which bedtime did I stop believing
my mother when she whispered,
"Safe and secure,"
and start wondering who she thought
she was kidding?

No particular epiphany.

Each day I stood there.
Eyes open, teeth clenched.

Waiting for dragons.

III.

The journey continues.
We have finished the kitchen and
dining room and are heading north
through the hall, leaving
midnight caves glimpsed only
by peering back towards
our point of embarkation.
For it is we who are Purveyors
of the Deep, Blue, Dark.

Not bad, I thought.
I closed my journal before
my baby sister Mary Ann smeared
red jelly over my purple prose.

Lulled by the rhythm of brush strokes
above, I lay on the floor and
watched my sister mountain climb
the sheet-covered furniture.
Saw my dad reach over and dab
her nose with blue.

He was doing O.K.!

Sometimes I shut my eyes
and listened to him becoming
Daddy again.
Heard his Tennessee-easy drawl
slide through stories we both knew
weren't true but, hey, that's the way
it should have happened.
After a while, he'd put his brush down,

"You gals could work a man to death,"

and go out on the back porch.
I'd sit with him
playing pat-a-cake with Mary Ann,
while he smoked a cigarette, and waited
for his hands to stop shaking.

Meanwhile, with or without us,
my mother painted on.

And I was getting worried.

She said,

"This blue should complement quite nicely
the mauve undertones in the living room
furniture."

What?

She said,

"Won't this shade enhance the accent tables
and the new bookcase?"

Wait a second.
Reality was no longer being spoken here.

I knew how much my mother hated
our dirty grey whale of a couch,
the fake-suede recliner stuck at half mast,
the tables (found "accenting" garbage cans
in the alley) and the bookcase
I autographed with a bobby pin
when I was six.

"Someday I'll get rid of all this junk"

had suddenly become,

"Keep everything covered - paint can
absolutely ruin fine furnishings."

The crazy thing was - I understood:

CURTAIN UP.
Hey, kids, let's put on a show!
Just hard work and some paint -
this place'll be a palace!

My mother's eternal search for a happy ending
by way of make-believe.
But I kept quiet.

Only their bedroom and the closets
were left. Only a major miracle
was needed.

Journal entry, Wednesday, 2:00 a.m.
Can't sleep
Sneak to living room.

White icebergs in a blue Arctic sea.
Slowly lift corner of sheet with toe.
See familiar frayed edge.
Return to bed,
disgusted with myself.
What did I expect -
an angel from Marshall Fields?
I mean, I've known for a long time -
whoever Jesus saves,
It isn't us.

IV.

Still, the next morning hits hard.

Brandishing a paintbrush, my mother sprints
down the hall yelling,

"You two quit dawdling - we're almost done!"

She pivots to a stop, lunges forward,
and with Captain Kidd precision, obliterates
a missed spot.

My father winks at me.
Lounging against the ladder,
his meticulous brushstrokes now
casual slaps, he's like a carefree drifter -
here to help the ladies out, and thanks
for the sandwich, ma'am, but, no,
never been the sort to settle down.

He whistles through his teeth.

She prowls for imperfections.

I take my worries and Mary Ann
to the park.

And come home to "Bye, Bye, Blackbird."
I peek in the living room.
There's my dad, pounding away on our
worn-out upright, while my mother
perches on top, touching up the trim,
swaying to the music. She throws a sultry
nightclub-singer-in-an-old-movie look
at the piano player and in wobbly harmony
they croon,

"Pack up all my cares and woes..."

I lean back out of sight.

So this is what they were like in the beginning.

I shut my eyes and pray hard:

O.K., forget the flashy stuff,
just let this go on.
One time, no disappointment,
let his go on.
A favor - kind of like the loaves and fishes.
So we can start over and over.
Rush Order: endless cans of #31 Lapis Lazuli -
Latex Flat. Leave in kitchen. On way out,
zap walls white. Amen.

I open my eyes.
The turpentine must be getting to me.
Mary Ann pulls at my jeans -
I pick her up, whisper, "Hush, hush,"
even though she isn't crying.

V.

Our Lady of Perpetual Paint must be napping -
we finish that afternoon.

Opening night jitters.

"Now don't come in 'til I call."

She's put on her Easter dress. Earrings.
Lipstick - half chewed off.
We listen to sheets being swooshed away,
living room furniture skidding,
while my father keeps clearing his throat
and Mary Ann fidgets.

It seems like hours.

"You can come in now."

But not long enough.

I rehearse my lines all the way
down the hall.

"No, Mom, you're wrong, it looks fine!
Honestly, everything looks..."

Fine.
Everything looks fine.
Maybe more than fine. Maybe lovely.

Cradled by the dusky walls,
our haphazard stuff seems -
chosen.
Burnished, not worn.
Antique mahogany, not old brown wood.
Aristocractic cracks, certainly not chips,
in her teacup collection.

Blue inked shadows baptize scratches.
Shabby is smudged to slightly faded
elegance.

"Allie, it's wonderful!"

My father whirls my mother off her feet.

"Mom, it's really fine," I shout.

Dumb word.

"I mean, it looks, it looks..."

"Cozy," my mother says, her eyes
for once triumphant, "Doesn't it look
cozy!"

And, though cozy isn't safe, oh,
it will do.

PULLING UP THE DAWN

by

HELEN G. REED

to my family

Some of the poems in this collection have appeared in little magazines. *Whetstone*, which published "Pregnant in the Embryology Lab," has nominated it for a Pushcart Prize XVII.

What a treat you, reader, have waiting for you! Helen Reed's poems are rich in language, used not for its own sake, but to embody a considerable range and depth of experience. Her poems will delight and enlighten you. They reveal what is often hidden from us in life's most heightened moments.

—Gary Pacernick

CONTENTS

Following her career in mental health, Helen Reed has found poetry a new way to say all she sees, and nature is never far away. Her poems have won several local literary awards.

She and her husband Art live in Evanston, Illinois, where they have a part-time antique business. They both enjoy bird-and-grandson watching.

photo credit: Larry Larimer

THE SNAPPING TURTLES

Years ago by motorboat we came,
my father, uncles, cousins and I,
roaring across the lake
to this wild place.
The motor throttled back, died.
We rode silence
into weed-clogged water.

With shattering clap
great water birds flew up,
hanging vines unlooped
and swam away.
Oarlocks creaked,
the wooden bottom boomed.
The men stood, leaned far out,
we children clinging to the sides.
They heaved up
from sucking marl and waterweeds
that cruel trap
laced with bait–
fish heads, entrails of pearl.
It had lured underwater giants
into its pronged wedge.

The trap shuddered with blows
of hissing prehistoric snouts,
snapping turtles of such age
their heads were big
as knotted fists.
They carried their past with them
in mossy gouts of green,
lost claws and lightning-forked
white scars on plated shells,
pale markings
of dark water gods.

The men, laughing, thrust sticks,
wrist-thick, into the trap
to see them cracked.
We trembled, hid our eyes, shrank
from monsters that we knew could
swim into our dreams that night.
Then the men drew the great heads
out of the shells,
jaws locked on stouter sticks,
and–still laughing–
chopped them off.

Years later, the channel tamed,
with willowed banks, we came,
a friend and I, to that same place.
In moonlight, by canoe,
we carved a golden path.
Then we stood, legs wide, balancing,
mounted the gunnels
and rocked and rocked–
moon dancers–
until we launched each other
in flying arcs
and splashed down into black.

Below the shattered crust we sank.
But we did not fear the darkness
of the monstered lake.

DAY OF YELLOW ROSES

Sleepless, I crept past
the half-open door where
my young aunt
slept, for the last time,
alone. Her wedding gown
hung in the hall–
shadows of lace–
near it, the handmade French hat
whose folds–soft insect wings–
curved down, clasped her face.

Who was that thief
who'd stolen her from us?
His careful little
ice cream advances pulled us
up the stairs of his laughter.

But she had let herself
be lured away, with her rose-scented
beads, sheet music songs
and trillia freshness of skin.

Where would I go
from this day on
when I woke in the night
and could not find my way
back into grey folds of sleep?
Would her door be closed
to me, hiding its secrets,
like that of my parents,
nesting in murmurs
across the hall?

At the kitchen table my father
hunched over coffee, then he and I
rasped across town
in the bitter-throated Model-T Ford.

In his friend's garden
he lifted me between the rows.
Drawn by a show as of moon,
we found the Talisman roses
my aunt would carry.

My father sliced stems, angling
the cut. Then, flowers on one arm,
me on the other, he walked back,
my long legs dangling
against his quick stride.

Through the car's window
he carefully laid
the weight of those roses
across my lap. The stems–
slashed from the only place
they had known–dripped ichor.
The streaming silk
wept fragrance.

Bitter almond filled my throat.
Then the sun flared up
and took the sky
and started us on
that long, long day.

THE QUIET CHILDREN

She trip-claws across
the kitchen floor,
my fawn-brown aunt,
quick as a passing thought,
shadowy as the spotted thrush
slipping into woodsy dark,
her lowered eyes flown
into lashes' thickets.
Withered arm hidden beneath
a homely apron, she is always
half-turned away from us.

We children sense
if you were to catch her–
with a splash of sunlight,
a shadow or whisper–
she'd wing for cover
with flutter and hop,
and–head tucked low–
she'd skim away.

Their farmhouse is a place of silence–
my large, smiling, scar-lipped uncle,
my scurrying, slippy, dark-eyed aunt.
How was it when their babies came
with cries and moans and helpless laughter?
Were their chucklings smothered with stillness,
were they swaddled in blankets of fog,
perhaps led to the woods
to learn the ways of quiet?

At the end of an afternoon at their pond
in the pasture, fishing in the green-scummed water
with my cousin from that quiet family,
I see my mother hurrying toward us.

Suddenly there is a quiet.
The switch-tailed, rolling-eyed cows
cease their mumbling and cudding.
A great form swings–head down–toward us
from the far end of the lane.

My mother's cry is strange and clotted–
squeezed from deep in her throat.
She seizes our arms, drags us and herself
over the fence, where we crouch and hide,
faces deep into pea leaves and pods.

As the bull comes nearer,
the earth beneath our faces
thrills to that dense tread.
We struggle not to cough from dust
flung up by the pocking hooves.
Pizzle-a-swish, he gallops.
We crouch deeper, and now the air
is rank, and there's a brutish reek
roiling up from those black flanks.

Breath whistles, gasped into his nostrils
with such a piercing shriek,
it's as if he is sucking from our lungs
the air we need to breathe.

Then, just the moment before
his massive darkness surges past,
I raise my head a little,
and I gaze on that old god–
his reddened eyes aglitter,
his swinging, mythic head crowned–
its horned moons at wax and wane.

My cousin already knew it.
But I learned stillness that day.

THE MICE

The hay, skewered
by curling prongs
of pitchfork,
revealed them there–
grey jelly beans,
their eyes still sealed,
their mouths just the size
for a mouse nipple–
tucked pod-tight
in fur-soft nest.

My cousin and I
scooped them up before
the fork
flashed down again.

We tried to eyedrop
milk into the tiny mouths,
and yet the litter's
inner brightness
embered down to ash,
as the babies dimmed,
one by one.

We took
a little matchbox,
lined it with cotton–
pulled out thin,
soft as marsh mist–
laid the tiny bodies in.

Their grave could not
have held a farmer's thumb,
but was just big enough
for small
whispery passings.

PULLING UP THE DAWN

Between midnight and summer dawn,
when I was very young, Father,
you often left my mother's bed
to drive into the unfurled night.
Then–if I awoke–from my room I'd hear
the screen door's creak, feel your leaving
bloom through the house.

I could picture you out there,
dark prince, in your watery world,
oars gliding over black ice,
playing your silvery games.

Great predators coiled among weeds,
waiting for the lure you arced, high,
to bring them flashing to the hook,
then the agonized, tail-slapping leap.

The fish twisted back through slippery stems
to break your line and steal the lure,
to return to their forever dusk
of palace spires below.

Caught, their magic melted away,
and they became like any other
stilled tame thing,
life's furious glitter dulled.

Oh, Father, I believed it was
your strong hook-flicking arm
pulled up the golden dawn
from below night's horizon.
For that reason I was able–
almost–to forgive you
for your leaving
so early and so often.

BURIED ALIVE

An icy hill at night,
the car veering, sliding
back down toward the brown
ridged fingers of water,
her mother at the wheel–
the girl, beside her, already gasping
for pearly bubbles of air, feeling
the black river seeping up
around her shiver
of pulled-in thighs,
the water a python,
swallowing a bird's
glitter-eyed panic flutter,
the girl hearing the splash
the car would make
as it entered the water,
began its slanted backward dive.

She tried not to
cry out. Then cried, "Jump!"
before she was trapped
with the mother, denied
her own breath.

She felt it–almost wanted it–
even as it did not
happen, the being sucked back up
into that narrow choke
of chute, held too closely
to the breast, nose buried
in the doughy sweetish flesh,
gasping, before she could
push out, force open the door against
the terrible drag of love.

And get away.

WILDNESS

After her mother's death she found it–
What a Young Man Ought to Know.
It was inscribed to her father from her mother
two years before their marriage.
"Early to bed, early to rise. No alcohol.
No smoking. Purity above all."

She could imagine her father
pulling it over his head
like a thick comforter in the night.
In his family little teaching had been done.
Life was lived as carelessly as pocket change
emptied out onto a bureau by the door.

The wonder was that she, Sleeping Beauty,
child of those two, ever awoke
to the faint china sound, the cracking
of a shell being pecked,
found the miniscule eaglet
of her own body's awakening
where it trembled below her heart.
Somehow she kept it hidden.

She slipped it crumbs from her own plate,
shreds of her own flesh;
felt it grow, flex its wings,
for that first flight.
The danger in it made her heart race,
kept her secretive as smoke.

When the boy who finally came and claimed her
got her to open her blouse, how she gasped
at the eagle's soaring–the bird's
great golden wings beating, glittering high above
where they struggled
in the storm's wild rush.

FATHER'S HOUSES

Blindfolded, I could walk through
a house, built by my father, listening, touching,
know it as his.

The notes that belled through domes
of rooms I'd sense were curtained
with light, as the oak front door
latched richly shut,
its scrolled brass plate
adding depth and weight
to that knelling swing.

That thick stunned thrust of hardwood
against soles of feet,
no easy careless give or creak,
echoes zigzagging in rooms
floored by terrazo, walled in tile,
heels' sharp grate on slate cellar steps.

The curved lines of marble fireplace
that surprises flesh
with coolness
even as it hints of heat,
sharp-edged marble sills at windows,
garden paths of herringboned bricks.

His marks upon the outer stone
where my fingers would know
his tool's chip, the cut and fit.

The houses were the way
I learned my father–
solid, giving shelter,
to be grown in,
not delicate,
but fine.

MOTHER'S THINGS

When she was younger she loved bits
of colored glass–a blue shoe,
hobbed, with hollow heels; a vase
as slippery yellow-green as vaseline.

Later, it was hammered silver
tea sets; worked and embroidered
table cloths; towels floating like clouds
above the steamy tub; and rugs–
so many hand-tied knots in each
that entire lives were woven, invisible,
among their flowers, vines and birds.

But, as she grew older, she reached
for what fitted in the hand

–a weighted trowel whose delicate probe
of snout could gentle out the tenderest bulb
without harm to brown parchment skin
or white fleshy heart;

–that scissors which curled itself
around her thumb and fingers
as if made of silk, molded there,
to sever flower stems
so that they wouldn't bleed;

–and the little paring knife
with hardwood handle,
its thin blade an aspen leaf
which trembles with first wind,
but which, curled in that hand,
could coax, peel, core
and slice
love
into a simmering pot.

DARK FLIRTATIONS

When her father's long white body
dove from the pier, it slapped
waves that surged away,
enlarging his shape
across the lake.

He plummeted down
into drop-off dusk.
Her heart's beat tried
to power
his pale arms and legs,
bring him–flailing–
into blue again.

She looked at her mother,
saw her mother's fingerprints
in the upper arms
where she'd folded herself
for comfort
while he–skinny
blowing whale–
heart-stroked back to them
in the hard waver
of their watching.

And now, years later,
a new man has come
to riffle her life by air,
as her father did by water.
She remembers her mother's
white fingerprints, the waiting.

In his plane, a yellow
butterfly in winter,
the new one dives upward
into dark skies.
On wings and struts too fragile,
he drives into black
air thick with fog that shrouds
the hills,
with cold that jewels ailerons
to ice.

Again, that old dark flirtation,
while she waits,
held iron-fast
by earth.

DU BARRY CUPS, CRANBERRY PLATES

When my mother's book club came for tea,
they'd travel to China and widen their eyes
over small girls with bound feet, crying slanted tears.
Or they'd cringe in the attic with Anne,
as Nazi soldiers tattooed at the door.

When the club ladies came back
from these adventures, eyes still smudged
from what they'd learned, they'd tilt
into the dining room to exclaim over cups
trellising roses, and click–with silver
stirrings–the bowls, amber with imported tea,
with pale lemon moons floating on top.

Cranberry plates glowed under cakes
sprouting violets, and when the ladies
blotted their scarlet lips, they'd butterfly
napkins that fluttered
down as softly as petals.

Mother's table had pulled her garden
inside–the blue-red of her early tulips,
as deep as cranberry glass; the pink
of the little roses and the sprawl
of take-over violets.

She would tip the teapot that matched the cups,
cat-back arch in her wrist.
"Du Barry Rose," she said sweetly each time,
in reply to their fluting queries.

When she was cocooned with gauzy eyes
and muffled ears, she dreamed–I like to think–
of her Du Barry cups, cranberry plates
and the bright, chirping cries
of Book Club ladies having tea.

COMFORT

She lies there,
shrunken into pastel quiet,
remote from summer's ribboned haze
and autumn's shine.

Now, by her willful act of dying,
she has tumbled me back into
her largeness, my smallness
again.

For a long time
she has been struggling
to escape
our needing her.

All those ruses!
That she didn't know us.
That she couldn't understand
she was in her own house
of fifty years.
The repeated calling out to go home
to her mama and papa,
to her childhood's place.

Now, my mother's child
inside me
peeks out,
sees her in the coffin,
resting, doing nothing,
wants to climb up,
slip into her arms one more time
and be rocked and rocked
into that comfort
she kept tucked
like a soft, fragrant sachet
on her breast.

WILD THINGS

Now that her dainty mother is dead,
she finds them everywhere–
minute glass and china
wild things,
captured in plastic
cylinders, in little bottles.

A china bear–
his salmon lungings,
berry roamings,
tree bark slashings–
is consigned
to the inside
of this tiny jar.

A rabbit rests alone
on a shred of netting
like a grey blur
of winter hedge.
His legs cannot hop.
He stares
through his round glass walls
with blue china eyes.

A fish no larger
than her littlest nail
swims like a smile
on its blue mirror.

All that's savage here
is brought down
to a scale so small
that it's tamed.

No wildness allowed!

Nothing leaps along
on legs
like springs
or swings freely
through the air.

This is not a place
where moans would ever tear
the middle of the night,
as the great golden carp
of delight
struggled upward
and flew glittering
high in moonlight,
while two figures twisted
below in the running river
of love.

Here, waters would be tamed
by dams and locks, and the fish
swim in exact, tiny, silver schools.

PUBERTY

When his daughter put on her bathing suit
for the first time that summer
her father noticed them there–
the two sharp, whorled shells–
pricking the top of the suit
from the delicate splay of her ribs.

With a catch in his chest
that he couldn't have named,
he remembered the slender
child she'd been,
who'd curled in his lap,
straddled his shoulders,
slept in his arms.

Now, as she ran toward him
to button the strap
he'd often helped with before,
he looked away.
She stopped, face broken
with confusion,
then turned to her mother.
His wife's look, a steely blade,
pressed down on him.

Now, one more time
each month, there'd be the faint
taint of old blood in the bathroom.
New geysers of feelings
would spout in the house
at imagined slights, would bubble,
hotly humid, around him. He longed for
cool white sheets
of paper, neat columns of figures,
his pencils lined in a row.

Instead, there'd be the cracked baying
of teenage boys on the porch,
a hint of jungles,
of stirred thick broths working
over the lick of low flames.

He remembered his sisters, the dark
musk beneath
the bright floral chords
of their perfumes,
the hard night beat
of his heart
until he'd escaped
that house.

THE WHISPERING CLOCK

A bud scale lies sloughed on the carpet
by some careless shoe. Gutters will soon
run red with that old blood of leaves
in this fevered time of catkins.

Called out by that flecked stain, by thudding
shutters and the ache of empty arms, I throw aside
wrinkled sheets, unsmoothed trowels, although
I know he'll be here soon, wanting dinner.

I'm drawn onto the scuff of rain-soaked earth
where a purple fledgling lies splayed–
beak wide, eyes scummed blue domes.

Far in the woods I'll find
a black and russet place.
There, in deepest pool,
jelled in jet, the eggs
of salamanders are clutches
of milky, moving orbs.

Beneath the horned owl's nest
twist tangles of fur, tiny bones
from swiftly, softly struck
small things, victims
of the shadow bird,
offerings to its young.

I want to turn away, go back inside
to whispering clocks, fine-cut glass,
have him find me busy there.
But I'd go lost in that one room,
be pulled in, sucked empty by its echoing walls,
hear the ghost rocking
of a cradle
that waits.

PREGNANT–IN THE EMBRYOLOGY LAB

Each week before I put on my white coat,
to stain and fix and slice,
I go to the shelf and look at them–
foetuses, each at a different stage,
submerged in their forever jars,
bottles enlarging from left to right.

I carry my own flesh-locked sea,
expanding around a cell cluster
that floats–shocked into growth
by the wriggling invader.

Soon there'll be the little
piggy thing, vestigial tail–
seahorse riding a tropical sea, rocking
near vessels branching bright as corals.

Next, he'll become the space visitor
waving filament hands, bulging eyes,
but blind in his dark capsule–
ectoplasmic head too big
for his wobbled stalk of neck.

At last there'll be a day
when the infant he's become–
last bottle on the right–
must leave his warm, round sac,
the lullaby of my heart.
And when he pushes out
into a premature sun,
bright oxygen will shock his lungs.

And even as he's flailing fists,
greedily tasting milky air,
too soon he'll run to know the wind.
I'll hear his seagull cry.

AFTER LOVE, BIOLOGY

The soft parts
of women
often end up
in the hard
hands of men
with knives.

They are then
discarded
into buckets
that clang
on cold, tile floors,
sections excised
for examination.

These parts,
once swimming
the warm hormonal
tides,
are reined in
by a ruddy moon.

How have things
drifted so far
from love
and its loose promises?

And what are they doing
there on that floor–
those lost,
soft
parts . . . ?

MICHAEL RECEIVING

Michael keeps an eye cocked on the universe
to see if black holes are imploding
or brown stars gathering heat.

When he walks he feels, through his soles,
deep underground the seep of water,
the long-ago shift and split of some great
buried plate of rock that once upthrust
into a jagged range, and slashed
a black-lightning rift in the plain.

Though almost six feet tall, Michael
hides the boy who inhabits the shell
of his too tuned-in body.
When he walks his garden with night,
the seeds–crackling, burst by swelling
shoots–tickle his thin-skinned toes.

In his sleep, he senses planetary misadventures–
the cries of ducks with oiled feathers,
caught by the fouled sea;
the despair of a child whose blood is invaded
by its own antic cells;
the slow deaths of lakes poisoned
by green skies raining ruin.

There is a humming in his ears from the horde
of signals pouring in. He sleeps uneasy dreams.

His body's a frail receptacle for this
universal static.
Still, his heart receives it all,
and mulls in elegant time
to the distant sighs
of the most
indifferent stars.

LOVE-FORTUNES

The family only whispered about
my grandfather's mother,
fierce little woman with heavy cane,
back bent like a boomerang, instead of pulling
up to the proud "I!" it must once have been.

I thought how she must have felt, walking,
looking at dirt–shuttling beetles, snails
trailing slime instead of flashing her eyes
at the gold line sealing two halves
of a midday sky or the sea edges of grain
running before the wind.

There was cause she walked that way,
they said, hooves, pounding the road
outside their village, galloping Cossacks
plunging in, the village women and girls
screaming, running through dust
and a tangle of legs–horses',
and leaping boots. The descending men,
tunics half–open, threw the girls down,
split open their thighs and rode away.

They left behind a girl who had danced
to see the spring woods go to lace;
who had told her love-fortune
in clouds in bright skies,
her skin bursting with honey,
like the berries that flamed by the road.

But that day dried her, left her soured
for the gentle older man she wed.
I say she let it bend her so she no longer
would have to see
the blue
lying sky.

AFTER THE FOOTBALL GAME

My grandson had been rising early,
I'd been told, lifting weights,
jogging, had grown thin,
moved away from the soft deer
grace of early adolescence.

I heard them first–the cadence
of the cleated feet,
then the leather gladiator slap
and scuff of shoulder pads,
the clank of helmets held
in young hands with great sprocketed
knuckles on the still-delicate arms.

I jumped back as the players
surged orange and white
through the gate,
bore down on me.
One broke stride, turned,
ran to my side, leaned down
and kissed me
with the face
of my young father.

HIDDEN SEED

by

LAUREL MILLS

in honor of Beth

CONTENTS

Photo credit: Lynn Koss

Laurel Mills lives in Neenah, Wisconsin, and teaches creative writing for the University of Wisconsin at the Oshkosh and Fox Valley campuses. She holds a B.A. in English and a M.A. in Humanities. Her first book of poems *The Gull Is My Divining Rod* (Wisconsin Review Press, 1985) won Outstanding Achievement honors from Wisconsin Library Association. Her second book *Canada Geese Coming Home* (Woelfinger Press, 1986) won an award from Council for Wisconsin Writers

JULY, PEASE POND, 1965

He and I are swimming,
have let ourselves over the side
of the blue skiff
into deep green water.
Far below us the muddy bottom
keeps secrets
of ancient turtles' lives.

We climb back in the boat.
Beads of water on our skin
disappear under the hot touch
of sun and hands.

The boat rocks us, rocks us,
we are rocking. His seed
swims inside me,
begins the journey
of the child we'll name Beth.

Already I hear her singing.
It's the oldest lullabye
she knows, the one my mother sang.
As she floats she carries
the memory of my dark eyes,
his full face.

He takes the rudder,
I stand in the bow.
Wearing his shirt,
I spread plaid wings
where blue dragonflies
glide in pairs.

THE NIGHT SHE IS BORN

One wrong moment in the womb
when cells meet,
a small breath missed
on the journey out,
a squeeze of forceps.

This night spins
with ether.
Beth struggles down
from the warm, safe place.
Her mouth sucks sharp air
into her cobweb lungs.

Her stick legs
are thrown into space.
I hear the doctor's slap, slap.
A long silence –

then her cry, faint as the sound
of mushrooms growing in a damp wood,
and the words that change our lives,
"This is a sleepy baby."

Outside, the world keeps spinning,
and a different child is here.

ON FINDING BETH IS RETARDED

The heaviness that wakes my night
I carry here to Cato Falls.
The sluggish river below
spits carp into the long
midday sun. Swallows fly
in and out of the limestone bank,
their shadows dart the river.

Spider webs gauze the ground,
catch wings in that first
upward flight. I'm anchored
at this riverbank, grieving
dreams I carried when she
soared in my womb.

Dreams of a dark-haired child
saying my name, dancing,
skipping rope.

Near the hollow base of an oak
I lift dead leaves,
see ants scurry with tiny eggs.
A helpless act of trying
to save their young.

All around me, webs
and sound of water moving.
I think of how long the river
has looped this limestone bank,
how swallows fly, how spiders
tether wings to the ground.

TEACHING BETH TO WALK

When she is two, we plant
the house with animal crackers.
They roar and bleat for her
to follow. Finally, we teach
her to crawl, to pull herself
up on the couch.

I call social workers,
surely they have tricks.
I scrub the house, bathe Beth,
set her in her pink high chair. But
when I let those two stiff women in,
Beth has stuffed her nose and ears
with chocolate cake.

I take her from doctor
to doctor. They pat my arm,
say, "Take her home and love her."
Could the stars burn hotter?
Already my love is greater than
light thrown from the sun.
Where have I failed
my little rubber legs,
my sleepy brain?

FALLING

I spend hours teaching Beth
to put a plastic star
in a five-pointed hole.
She always chews the star.

Her dad curls her fingers
around a spoon, lifting hand
to alphabet soup, to mouth
over and over again.
She drops the spoon.

Then, as she lies mesmerized
by the overhead light,
he bicycles her floppy legs.
For traction, he puts adhesive tape
on the soles of her shoes,
walks her back and forth.

When he takes his hands from hers,
she stands a moment,
then sinks.
Our shooting star
disappearing down a dark sky.

A NEW BABY TO MEND US

In October when geese cut the sky,
we bring the new baby home.
Her blonde head alert,
she straightens strong legs,
digs her feet in my lap.

We call this child Marissa.
To barricade her from Beth's
jealous orthopedic shoes,
we prop her inside a playpen
surrounded by stuffed rabbits.

Beth, three and newly walking,
paces the perimeter of the mesh walls,
a lion shut out of its den.
For months, gripping the plastic rail,
she bites a floppy ragdoll, stomps it,
pretends it's her baby sister.

Finally Beth plops down,
pushes her nose against the net,
fascinated that this round thing inside
knows her. When she waves her hands,
Marissa lifts her fat arms.
"Ya-Ya," Beth says.

Even when she grows old enough
to have her own babies, Beth will
carry a blonde doll she calls "Ya-Ya."
She'll cover her with band-aids, stick
a thermometer pencil in her mouth,
and press on her chest
to make the rubber heart beat.

DEER AT SUNSET

Clouds swallow sun.
In a scalped hayfield
seven pair of deer lips
curl back at a crippled buck.
Does and fawns snort,
stamp their feet until
he stumbles back into a cornfield.

My heart pulls back remembering
the neighbor that wouldn't let
her kids outside
when Beth was in the yard,
those boys that screamed,
"Retard!" and put wax
paper on the playground slide,
pushed Beth on that wild ride.

When her face hit the pavement,
lips split like red clouds.

Tonight inside this bleeding sunset
deer go on feeding
like neighbors pulling drapes
on our side of the house,
locking the back gate.

SISTERS DRESSING UP

It is that moment
before their lives turn –
that one carefree moment
before the cedar waxwing
falls from the sky,
drunk on mountain ash berries.

Marissa, at three, wears heavy skirt
and oversize shoes
in the same way she will one day
learn to wear perfection.
She dresses six-year-old Beth
as if she were a mannequin,
a large doll with a hollow mind.

She makes Beth's face
with eye shadow and rouge.
Kneels on the floor
and lifts her feet
into battered high heels.
Fastens a discarded rhinestone
necklace around Beth's throat.
Drapes fake fur
on her shoulders.

Now she has dressed them both.
Marissa takes Beth's hand,
leads her outside
down the steps.
Sunlight falls
on their heads,
their bobbing hats.

HOOKED ON THE WORLD SERIES

In Beth's bed
a blue baseball cap
angles above dark lashes
that fringe her dreams.

Eggshell eyelids twitch
at the toss of a white ball
on a field where
she makes the team.

Bubbles rise in her drool
like baseballs soaring
in an endless sky,
weightless,
free.

As I bring the blanket
to her chin, I grin
remembering how she
stopped traffic
at the supermarket entry

doing an instant replay
of a TV homerun:

slow lift of her arm
slow roll of the leg
slowly   sliding
through open doors.

AT THE END OF CHURCH STREET

Ken bends the day harvesting tomatoes,
dries them on the front porch.
When he steps inside for iced tea,
Beth bites each one. He comes back
to thirty-seven red mouths gaping.

I rush money over but he just laughs,
says something about tomato stew,
about our being new in the neighborhood.

Then Beth takes a swipe with white
paint on the red shed he spent
all spring building. He chuckles,
gives her a bucket, shows her
how to pluck eggs.

Every morning, she barrels into Ken's
house for his wife's banana bread.
Then they walk to the barn,
Beth bragging, "Me help Ken eggs!"

From then on, every important man
in her life will be Ken: bus driver,
fireman, and at Lion's Camp
when the counselor asks
kids to call out their names
she yells, "KEN!"

Long after Beth moves away
she dreams of a bald man
opening his hands, a yellow chick
hatching.

WILD DAYS

Beth kneels at my bed and pries my eyes,
"Up, Mama! Up!" I wrap the scratchy wool
of dark dawn around me, but soon
I'm dragged awake by the Gingerbread Man
screeching at the top of his phonograph lungs.

Beth stands on a wooden toybox, bangs
on a beat-up guitar. Milk covers Cheerios
in a gallon tupperware bowl, a five-pound
bag of sugar frosts the countertop.
While the rest of us eat, she thinks
her father's cheek a hollow tree
and pokes, pokes, pokes. A hole bores
under his beard at her woodpecker finger.

Then she tears out of the house in football
helmet and plastic goggles, sees her sister
sitting on the lawn shooting marbles,
rides her bike up Marissa's back.
The kids sneak into a neighbor's house, but
Beth tracks them down, bashes through the door
yelling, "Missa go home. Missa home!"

At home Beth cranks up Flintstones, tries
to unsnarl the rope we've tied around
the gold refrigerator. I button my earflaps
with wine and valium. Her sister
weeps in her yellow room. Her dad floats
in his boat in the quiet garage. He broods
over the salmon he caught, how it
bent the pole, pulled the line taut –
snapped.

SENDING BETH AWAY

In the court corridor
her dad stares at his feet.
I press my trembling back
against the wall.
Has someone taken
a piano wire
and worked it through
all the places I carried her:
womb, heart, head?

When the bailiff calls us,
we lead Beth to the courtroom.
Recognizing Perry Mason benches,
she says, "Oh, no.
Me no go to jail!"
Her dad takes her left hand,
I take her right. We walk through
the wooden gate.

We three sit at a long table.
The judge asks,
"Beth, would you like
to live in a group home?"
Her bewildered doe eyes
look to me, to her dad.
She stands, clutches
her Mickey Mouse backpack
and says the only thing
that makes any sense to her,

"Me no pee in the shower!"

WHEN BETH IS FIRST AWAY

When I pass Beth's room,
I know the mourning dove
returning to its nest
to find its young is missing.

I know quiet.
One down feather
falling to grass.
Beth's bed unslept in.

All night I hear
sounds she used to make.
That little gurgling
in her sleep, padding
to bathroom in the dark.

Outside my window the dove
circles its empty nest.
Swoops from phone wires
to branches, downspouts.

In early morning
the dove is gone.
Looking at the cedar
where it used to sit,
I think of Beth waking

miles away
calling for me.

GONE TO A HOME FOR RETARDED

This is the age Beth should be
eating chocolates,
talking to girl friends.
Chairs in the living room
should wear her sweaters.
A boy should arrive
in a green Chevy,
take her for pizza and movies.

I should wait up as the clock
crawls past her curfew,
yell at her for making me worry,
threaten to ground her.

Marissa should sit on her bed
after the lights go out,
tell how the boy she likes
keeps ignoring her.
Beth should give
older-sister advice
on sex, tampons,
and smoking in the garage.

Instead, we have closed the door
to her empty room. We wait
this long month
for our first visit
to her group home.
Every day I open the door,
see the corner
where her guitar stood,
the doll impression on her bed,
the dust where her record player
sang on the dresser.

IN A BRICK HOUSE ON KOEHLER

At fifteen, Beth is learning
to make salads.
Every night, slicing celery,
she pretends to cut her finger
so she can wear a band-aid.
She sets the table,
matching forks and spoons
to the drawing on the placemats.

Mornings, she makes her bed,
spread hanging sideways,
pillow case half off,
then helps feed applesauce
to the boy with cerebral palsy.

She brings her roommate
crayons to calm her.
When she needs calming herself,
she leans her head against the wall
in a five minute time-out.

On Saturday night she taps
her lap to rock and roll,
while college-age helpers
swing kids in wheelchairs and walkers.
She won't dance yet, but
one foot moves to the music.

THE A.R.C. PLAYS BASEBALL

Beth is seated on the bench
wearing mask and catcher's
belly mat, her hat on backwards.
When the game begins,
she surrenders these,
watches through the wire fence.
All summer she has sat here.

This last game of the season
the coach sways her to play.
All the way to home plate
she insists, "Me no bat!"

Her legs locked in a stance,
bat over her shoulder,
she waits.
One small spirit in the universe.

The white ball leaves
the pitcher's hand, soars,
a shadow on the sun.

It drops, floats toward her
like an apple blossom falling
from a dark tree.

Beth swings: up, down like an axe.
When the ball flies past,
she cries, "Me mad!"
But as she turns,
retarded men and women cheer
for the wild miss, that lunge.

WOOD WALKING WITH BETHY

This pine branch has taken the shape
of a straw broom. I would sweep
this forest floor for my daughter,
would hack away piercing limbs.
But I can only watch her
bend and push her way.

I spot a bluejay feather on the ground.
"Bethy, see this! And here are three more.
We could piece together a whole bird,"
I laugh, sticking them in her pocket.

We leave the pine grove, walk to a small
brook. "Listen to the water gurgle, Bethy.
There are trout under that rock."
She smiles in her vacant way.
It is enough for her just to be with me.
But I want to give her this other.

"Oh, Bethy, see the butterfly," I whisper
as we scare up a monarch. She nods, but
has missed it. As we cross a footbridge,
I point, "A waterfall down there."
She puts her hands on her hips,
announces emphatically, "Steep hill!"

On her birthday last month I sang to her.
I would not sing for anyone else. Nineteen
years ago she sang inside my womb. Now
I kneel on the footbridge, pick up a fragile
blue cup, fold it into her hand.
"Robin's egg, Beth."

WAITING FOR BETH'S SURGERY

I want the great lake to offer me
its endless brushing of shore.
I drag my weariness to its beach
like a dead fish to be washed away.
I am alone here. Only a tern flaps
a shadow against white birches
in the dunes behind me.

It is letting her go under
that worries me. As if
I hadn't let go enough,
again and again.

In her deep sleep the surgeon
will slice near those delicate
bones, those tiny shells,
where the motion of fluid
carries sound.

Will she hear her name
when I breathe it to her,
"Beth, Beth, Bethy?"

I do not want to see
these weeds the lake has swept up,
tangled on driftwood like hair
of a drowned girl.

Instead I kneel at a gull's nest
in the sand, laid so tenderly
with the gull's own down
as if to hold
the most fragile egg.

HEALING

Driving Beth to the hospital
I see sun rising,
sheen on corn stubble
waiting to be turned under.

As she's wheeled to the operating bay
I take her hand, tell her
about the mask and the deep
sleep. She never questions me.

In the waiting room, I hold
a cup for warmth, gaze into coffee
rich as Beth's eyes. In an unexpected
moment of surrender
I set my cup down, trust
the eye of the clock
to blink out time.

Days later I'm packing Beth,
balloons, flowers in my car
when suddenly we hear
a great trumpeting.
Above us, wild swans
arc all at once,
sheen on their wings.

BIKING ON SHADY LANE

My eyes follow
a hawk circling the sun
and my twenty-year-old daughter
intent on making her feet go around.

After a while, I stop for breath
but Beth keeps pumping.
Some said she'd never learn.
Her dad taught her,
strapped her feet to the pedals,
pushed her with his long frame.

He trained her flaccid fingers
to grip handlebars, her feeble
legs to make a circle.
He spent months wheeling her
back and forth on a small bicycle.

Over the years she's snapped
her collarbone, worn a stapled
zipper on her forehead,
cracked her eye glasses.
And always climbed
back on her bike.

Today there's a flash of red
tail as the hawk, intent
on a field mouse, spirals down.
Though I'm tired, ready
to turn back, Beth pedals harder.
Against the sun I see
her head bent,
legs circling.

WORK, HERS AND MINE

I scour Lake Michigan for poems
while at school Beth learns work.
She didn't walk until she was three.
Now she carries newspapers to 63
houses, her hands black with ink.
The teacher dogs her tracks
warning her to lift her head
at street corners.

I cross the sand, remember the year
she buried her beachball and we dug
hole after hole searching for it.
She brings that same insistence
to scrubbing bathroom floors,
cafeteria tables.

Once she sat for hours
and hurled stones into the lake,
leaving a bald place around her.
Now she sits and fits washers
on a wooden peg, collates pages.
These tasks are not too small.

When asked if she likes her jobs,
she says, "Yes, me no fired."
When the lake whispers do I love her,
I say, "Yes, I am proud."

I draw her name on the beach.
She painstakingly prints it
on the back of a check.
And this red stone at my feet
is my heart the lake tosses up to her.

LINCOLN SCHOOL GRADUATION

In this gym, therapeutic trampolines
and leg braces have been
pushed aside for the hundred of us
come to applaud
and to get something to hold
in our own dark nights.

The music starts and the boy
with the flag makes a wrong turn.
The four graduates march in:
a speechless girl in a wheelchair,
an autistic boy,
Beth with roses on her wrist,
and the boy she always dances with.

She spots me in the front row,
calls out, "Me big presents?"
I nod and smile.
She finds her seat on stage.
When her name is called –
Beth Marie Mills –
she stands to the cheering and,
for a girl who never learned to cry,
her own new tears.
In this complete moment I forgive
the doctor who declared
she'd never be anything.

As music pulls graduates
down the middle aisle,
I catch her dad's full eyes,
her blonde sister smiling.
Linking us: this child
and the tassled cap.

BETH'S FRIENDS AND THEIR BABY

Paul hands Beth the child.
She holds him awkwardly and,
in some buried maternal pond,
finds the instinct to pat him.

Paul catches the image
in a camera: Beth and baby.
Behind my lashes, a picture of me
two decades ago, holding her.

Beth rocking this child,
shadow me rocking her.
I see both in the same way
a snowy egret balances
on its own white reflection.

BJ brings a bottle, helps Beth
position the baby in crook of arm,
nipple in his puckered mouth
so the white liquid flows.

Beth's eyes reflect the glow of ash
in the wood stove. Her dark head
sways as she coos and rubs
the baby's back in circles.
In the window behind her
rocks the moon's empty cradle.

THE SISTERS FLY TO GRANDMA'S

"You boss, Missa?" Beth fidgets
in the plastic chair as she
asks her younger sister,
"Me ride stairs, okay Boss?
Go up, down, twenty times."

In the long wait for the flight
Marissa reads a teenage romance.
At the end of every paragraph
she lifts grey eyes to the escalator,
her sister ascending.

When their flight is called,
she leads Beth to the gate.
"Fix my ny'ons," Beth says,
lifting her skirt and tugging.
Marissa pulls the dress back
into place, then leads her
to the jet-way.

On the plane Beth wants
to sit alone. But Marissa
settles beside her, whispers,
"I'm the boss, remember?"

"Me do homework," Beth says, pulling
worn spiral and pen from her backpack.
"Study, fifty-five minutes!"
Her dark head bends over
the blank page. Marissa's blonde hair
rests against the seat. The plane
lifts, swallowed by fog.

BETH SPEAKING

Ah, um, I talk you.
I go work.
My group home go bus.
Quarter in hole.
My job. Knives, forks,
spoons in box.
Boss lady say,
"Beth, no talk."
Me work hard.
Hot sweat.
No little kid no more.
Woman. Biggg!
I go work.
Take break my friends.
Pack my lunch.
Ham, cheese, chips.
Pop in 'chine. Quarter.
Boss lady say,
"OK, talk."
Go my group home. Bus.
Wait...me thinking.
Like my job.

AT FOX RIVER MALL

In sunset the glass panels
of the mall are tinted.
The city beyond grows
dark spirals and peaks.
I people-watch while
waiting for the movie theater
to open its ticket gate.
In the flurry of gliding shoppers
Beth walks by.

She seems like someone else's
grown-up child, hair permed,
purse over her shoulder.
I know the group home aide
guides her path
and Beth will insist,
"Change, please, 55 cents!"
to the next shopkeeper
no matter what the cost.

Rising to call to her,
I suddenly think of the eagle
that lines its nest with thistle,
spurring its young to fly.

I watch her move
in the pink sun.